VIRGINIANS' INVENTIONS

After the American Revolution, **Virginia's agricultural base** begins to change. **Tobacco** farming is hard on the soil, causing many to look for new ways to grow crops or for new jobs to do. **Thomas Jefferson** and **Cyrus McCormick** invent better farming tools. **Lewis Temple** helps others farm the seas. Other Virginians turn their creative problem-solving skills to other areas . . .

D1546995

WHAT DID THOMAS JEFFERSON INVENT?

VIRGINIA HAS SEEN SOME GREAT INVENTORS IN ITS TIME. LET ME SHOW YOU SOME!

Thomas Jefferson IS PROBABLY THE GREATEST VIRGINIA INVENTOR.

AS MINISTER TO FRANCE IN THE 1780s, JEFFERSON FALLS IN LOVE WITH FRENCH AND ITALIAN FOOD. WHEN HE COMES BACK TO VIRGINIA, HE DESIGNS A MACARONI MAKER!

HE ALSO INVENTS A SUN DIAL THAT CAN TELL TIME TO WITHIIN A MINUTE OR TWO OF THE REAL TIME.

IT CAN BE TWISTED TO WORK AT ANY LATITUDE ON EARTH.

YOU KNOW WHAT WOULD MAKE THIS REALLY GOOD? SOME BRIGHT ORANGE CHEESE!

WORKING AS SECRETARY OF STATE FOR THE UNITED STATES, JEFFERSON MAKES A SECRET CODING DEVICE! IT HAS 26 ROWS OF LETTERS TO SCRAMBLE AND UNSCRAMBLE MESSAGES!

IN 1794, JEFFERSON MAKES A MOLDBOARD TO GO BEHIND A PLOW. IT MAKES DEEPER ROWS THAN THE ONES FARMERS HAD BEEN USING. THIS REDUCES SOIL EROSION ON FARMS IN VIRGINIA'S PIEDMONT REGION.

AND THAT LEADS US TO OUR NEXT INVENTOR...

NEXT: THE SLIM REAP

BOYD '01

2

WHAT DID CYRUS McCORMICK INVENT?

A VIRGINIAN CREATES ONE OF THE GREATEST FARMING INVENTIONS EVER (BEFORE THE TRACTOR, OF COURSE!).

CYRUS McCORMICK

IS BORN IN 1809 IN WESTERN VIRGINIA. HIS FATHER MAKES FARM TOOLS. HE HAS TRIED FOR YEARS TO INVENT A MACHINE TO HARVEST WHEAT.

ONE FARMER SWINGING A BROAD SCYTHE CAN CUT ONLY TWO ACRES OF WHEAT IN A HARD DAY'S WORK.

HURRY UP, McCORMICK! MY ARM IS GETTING TIRED!!

BOYD'01

RATS!! CYRUS, DO YOU HAVE ANY IDEAS??!

WITH THE HELP OF SLAVE JO ANDERSON, CYRUS McCORMICK MAKES A MECHANICAL REAPER THAT DOES WHAT HAND TOOLS DO SEPARATELY.

HAKLAKLAKFLAKHAWAKLAKWAKLAK

IT'S TOO LOUD! IT'S SCARING THE HORSE!

OVER THE NEXT SEVERAL YEARS, McCORMICK IMPROVES HIS DESIGN. A KNIFE MOVES THROUGH FIXED ROWS TO CUT THE GRAIN, WHICH FALLS INTO A BASKET.

WHEEEE! NOW WE CAN CUT 12 ACRES A DAY — WHILE WE ARE SITTING DOWN!!

WHO IS SITTING DOWN?

THIS REAPER WILL LET FARMERS GROW WHEAT IN THE HUGE PRAIRIE LEWIS AND CLARK FOUND BEYOND THE MISSISSIPPI RIVER!

McCORMICK'S REAPER DOUBLES THE AMOUNT OF WHEAT ONE PERSON HARVESTS. IT MAKES AMERICA "BREADBASKET OF THE WORLD" — AND, LATER, "CHEERIO BOWL OF THE WORLD."

next: HARPOON LEW'S

WHO MADE A BETTER WHALE HARPOON?

A VIRGINIAN INVENTS AN IMPORTANT TOOL IN THE HISTORY OF AMERICAN WHALING.

LEWIS TEMPLE IS BORN A SLAVE IN RICHMOND IN 1800. BY 1829 HE HAS ESCAPED TO NEW BEDFORD, MASSACHUSETTS. IT IS A CITY WHERE MOST PEOPLE WORK IN THE WHALING TRADE.

WHALE OIL IS USED TO LIGHT LAMPS IN THE EARLY 1800s. BUT CATCHING A WHALE IS A RISKY BUSINESS...

NO! HE'S GETTING AWAY!

THESE STUPID HARPOONS PULL OU OF THE WHALE'S SKIN TOO EASILY

LEWIS, WE LOST 11 WHALES ON OUR LAST VOYAGE.

TEMPLES BLACKSMITH SHOP Since 1836

TRY THIS. I USED MY IRONWORKING SKILLS TO MAKE A TOGGLE HARPOON. WHEN THIS POINT ENTERS THE WHALE, IT TURNS TO LOCK IN.

BOYD '01

TEMPLE'S 1848 INVENTION MAKES CATCHING WHALES MUCH EASIE HIS HARPOON IS SOON USED ON ALMOST ALL WHALING SHIPS.

HE DOES NOT PATEN HIS HARPOON. PEOPL CAN COPY HIS IDEA WITHOUT PAYING HIM TEMPLE DIES IN 185

NEXT: PATHFIND

WHAT DID MATTHEW MAURY CREATE?

THIS VIRGINIAN STARTS A NEW WAY OF THINKING ABOUT THE OCEANS.

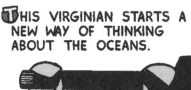

MATTHEW F. MAURY

IS BORN NEAR FREDERICKSBURG IN 1806. HE JOINS THE UNITED STATES NAVY AT AGE 18. BUT A STAGECOACH ACCIDENT DISABLES HIM. HE CANNOT BE A FIGHTING SAILOR ANYMORE. WHAT NOW?

MAURY IS ASSIGNED TO THE NAVY'S DEPOT OF CHARTS AND INSTRUMENTS.

HERE IS ANOTHER ONE OF THOSE BORING LOGBOOKS YOU MAKE THE CAPTAINS FILL OUT ON THEIR TRIPS.

SPAIN

U.S.

ATLANTIC OCEAN

AFRICA

MEXICO

GREAT! MAPPING THE OCEAN'S WINDS AND SEA CURRENTS WILL SHORTEN VOYAGES.

LOOK AT THE GULF STREAM. THERE IS A RIVER IN THE OCEAN!!

IN 1855, MAURY WRITES "PHYSICAL GEOGRAPHY OF THE SEA." IT IS THE FIRST MODERN BOOK OF OCEANOGRAPHY — THE STUDY OF LIFE UNDERWATER.

MAURY ALSO CHARTS THE ATLANTIC OCEAN FLOOR.

Atlantic Ocean Depths

ENGLAND

FRANCE

SPAIN

I HAVE DISCOVERED A PLATEAU FROM NEWFOUNDLAND TO IRELAND. WE CAN LAY A TRANSATLANTIC CABLE THERE FOR SENDING TELEGRAPH MESSAGES TO EUROPE.

THE FIRST COMMUNICATION CABLE BETWEEN NORTH AMERICA AND EUROPE IS LAID IN 1858.

AMERICA'S CIVIL WAR BEGINS IN 1861, MAURY JOINS THE CONFEDERATE NAVY.

HOW ARE YOU DOING WITH THAT NEW ELECTRIC TORPEDO?

SHH!

HAVE YOU INVENTED AN ELECTRICAL MINE TO GUARD OUR HARBORS YET??

SHHH!

HIS WORK WILL BE IMPORTANT TO OTHER NATIONS IN LATER WARS.

MAURY DIES IN 1873.

NEXT: THE FEVER

WHO DISCOVERED YELLOW FEVER'S CAUSE?

A VIRGINIAN SWATS A REALLY BIG PROBLEM 100 YEARS AGO...

BZZZZ

WALTER REED

IS BORN IN 1851 IN GLOUCESTER COUNTY. THIS SON OF A MINISTER JOINS THE ARMY MEDICAL CORPS IN 1875.

IN THE 1800s, SOUTHERN PORTS IN THE UNITED STATES LOSE THOUSANDS OF PEOPLE TO "YELLOW FEVER." FOR EXAMPLE, AN 1855 OUTBREAK OF THE DISEASE KILLS MORE THAN 2,000 PEOPLE IN NORFOLK.

KEEP THAT TAR BURNING! IT PURIFIES THE DIRTY AIR.

WRONG SOLUTION! WE MU[ST] CLEAN ALL SHIPS COMING HERE FROM SOUTH AMERIC[A] THEY CARRY THE FEVER!!

IN THE SPANISH-AMERICAN WAR IN 1898, MORE SOLDIERS DIE FROM YELLOW FEVER THAN FROM BATTLEFIELD INJURIES.

REED, WHAT CAUSES THIS?

DOES IT SPREAD BY TOUCHING??

BY SHARING CLOTHES?

OLD SMELLY MATTRESSES?

GETTING KISSED BY A DOG??

IT IS CARRIED BY MOSQUITOES. KILL THEM AND YOU KILL

REED'S YELLOW FEVER COMMISSION IS THE FIRST TO PROVE THAT MOSQUITOES CARRY YELLOW FEVER. THIS DISCOVERY ALLOWS OTHER SCIENTISTS TO FIND A VACCINE IN 1937.

IT ALSO ALLOWS THE U.S. TO DIG THE **PANAMA CANAL** THROUGH A HOT JUNGLE BY FIRST DESTROYING MOSQUITO BREEDING PLACES.

THE LAST YELLOW FEVER EPIDEMIC IN THE U.S. IS IN NEW ORLEANS IN 1905.

MAGGIE LENA WALKER

Black Americans have trouble using their rights in the time between the **Civil War** and **World War II**. **"Jim Crow" laws** make it hard for them to vote or mix with white people in public. Despite this, **Richmond's Maggie Lena Walker** finds a way to help black people make **economic choices** for themselves . . .

WHERE DID MAGGIE WALKER LIVE?

CHESTER! HELP ME HIDE! BULLY IS TRYING TO TAKE MY MONE

QUICK, TAMARA — BEHIND THIS DOOR!

WHOOP
WHERE ARE WE?!

WE'RE IN THE HOME OF **MAGGIE LENA WALKER**. IN 1902. SHE IS A BLACK LEADER IN RICHMOND, VIRGINIA.

HELLO, CHILD. ARE YOU HERE TO JOIN THE INDEPENDENT ORDER OF ST. LUKE?

WHAT IS THAT??

IT IS A GROUP ORGANIZED TO HE ITS MEMBERS. A PERSON PAYS MONTH DUES TO ST. LUKE. THE GROUP US THAT MONEY TO HELP ANY MEMBE WHO IS SICK OR TOO OLD TO WO

OUR JUVENILE BRANCH THROWS PARTIES, TALENT SHOWS, AND PARADES TO TEACH YOUNG PEOPLE TO HELP THEMSELVES.
"JUST AS THE TWIG IS BENT, THE TREE'S INCLINED."

ACTUALLY, I NEED HELP. I NEED A SAFE PLACE TO KEEP MY ALLOWANCE FROM A BULLY.

WHAT YOU NEED IS A BANK.

A BANK HMMMM

next: INTERDEPENDENCE DA

WHAT DOES A PRODUCER DO?

CHESTER AND THIRD-GRADER TAMARA ARE IN RICHMOND, VIRGINIA, IN 1902 . . .

MAGGIE WALKER, CAN YOU HELP ME HIDE MY ALLOWANCE?

YOU DON'T HIDE MONEY. YOU SAVE IT IN A BANK!

THE FIRST BANK IN AMERICA CHARTERED BY BLACKS BEGAN IN RICHMOND. IN 1888 THE SAVINGS BANK OF THE GRAND FOUNTAIN UNITED ORDER OF TRUE REFORMERS OPENED.

IN 1902, RICHMOND IS ONE OF AMERICA'S BEST PLACES FOR BLACKS TO RUN A BUSINESS. THERE ARE BLACK-OWNED SHOE STORES, RESTAURANTS, NEWSPAPERS . . .

WE RICHMOND BLACKS ARE INTERDEPENDENT. THAT MEANS WE NEED EACH OTHER TO GET GOODS AND SERVICES. EACH ONE OF US IS A PRODUCER AND CONSUMER. PRODUCERS MAKE THE CLOTHES OR COOK THE FOOD THAT PEOPLE DEMAND. THOSE WHO USE THE FOOD OR SERVICES ARE CONSUMERS.

WE BLACKS DO THIS BECAUSE WE HAVE TO. WHITES PASS MORE JIM CROW LAWS EVERY YEAR. WHITES WILL NOT LET US EAT AT THE SAME RESTAURANTS AS THEY DO, GO TO THE SAME SCHOOLS, OR RIDE THE SAME TROLLEY SEATS.

EVER SINCE I BECAME LEADER OF THE INDEPENDENT ORDER OF ST. LUKE IN 1899, I HAVE URGED OUR MEMBERS TO BUY BLACK.

I GOT ST. LUKE TO START A NEWSPAPER AND CLOTHING STORE. NOW WE'LL START A BANK FOR YOUR MONEY.

BOYD'01

next:
PENNY CANDY

WHAT COULD A PENNY BUY IN 1902?

CHESTER AND TAMARA ARE IN 1902 RICHMOND:

A BANK? UMMM, WELL, MAYBE I COULD JUST SPEND MY ALLOWANCE. IS THERE A MOVIE THEATER HERE?

WE DO NOT HAVE MR. EDISON'S FANCY MOTION PICTURES AROUND HERE YET.

HOW ABOUT SOME ICE CREAM THEN? SOME POPCORN?

ROBERTSON'S EMPORIUM of ECONOMIC CHOICES

THOSE ARE TWO ECONOMIC CHOICES WE DO HAV

HELLO, JOHN.

WHAT ARE YOU CHOOSING TODAY??

I EARNED A PENNY FROM DELIVERING LAUNDRY. I AM TRYING TO DECIDE BETWEEN BUYING A WHISTLE, THREE COOKIES, OR A LOLLIPOP.

I GUESS I'LL GET COOKIES.

JOHN MADE AN ECONOMIC CHOICE. PICKING COOKIES MEANS NOT GETTING A WHISTLE OR LOL POP TODAY. MISSING THE WHISTLE AND LOLLIPOP HIS OPPORTUNITY COST. TO BUY THEM HE MU CARRY MORE LAUNDRY TO EARN ANOTHER PENNY.

HOW ABOUT YOU, TAMARA?

ALL SHOES $1

WOW! ONLY A NICKEL FOR A DRINK? I HAVE $3 - I COULD DRINK ALL DAY!

AND YOU WOULD BE SICK ALL NIGHT. YOU MIGHT WANT TO SAVE YOUR MONEY TO BUY SOMETHING MORE EXPENSIVE LATER.

OK. I'LL GET JUST ONE DRINK TODAY AND PUT THE REST IN YOUR NEW BANK.

YOU'LL FIND IT INTEREST-ING!

next: FRE MONE

HOW CAN YOU GET FREE MONEY?

MAGGIE LENA WALKER RUNS THE INDEPENDENT ORDER OF ST. LUKE IN RICHMOND, VIRGINIA, IN 1903...

WELCOME TO THE NEW ST. LUKE PENNY SAVINGS BANK!

I THINK WE WILL BRING IN MORE THAN $9,000 THIS FIRST DAY.

MRS. WALKER, I HAVE COME FROM NEW YORK JUST TO PUT MY MONEY IN YOUR BANK. I WANT MY MONEY TO HELP OTHER BLACK PEOPLE.

THANK YOU. WE WILL TURN YOUR NICKELS INTO DOLLARS.

HOW DOES SHE DO THAT?

A BANK IS A BUSINESS THAT MANAGES MONEY. MAGGIE WALKER TAKES MONEY FROM THE FIRST MAN'S SAVINGS ACCOUNT AND **LOANS** IT TO OTHER PEOPLE AND BUSINESSES. THE LOAN HELPS THEM BUILD STORES, GET AN EDUCATION, TAKE VACATIONS...

OVER TIME, PEOPLE OR BUSINESSES REPAY MAGGIE WALKER THE AMOUNT OF MONEY THEY BORROWED — PLUS **INTEREST**. INTEREST IS THE FEE THE BANK CHARGES FOR MANAGING MONEY.

THE BANK PAYS PART OF THAT INTEREST BACK TO THE FIRST MAN. EXTRA INTEREST MONEY IS HIS REWARD FOR KEEPING HIS SAVINGS AT MAGGIE WALKER'S BANK.

FREE MONEY — IT'S A BETTER RETURN THAN BURYING YOUR MONEY IN A HOLE!

SIGN ME UP! HERE IS MY **DEPOSIT**

MAGGIE WALKER IS THE FIRST BLACK WOMAN PRESIDENT OF A CHARTERED BANK IN AMERICA. DEPOSITS IN ST. LUKE GROW FROM $103,000 IN 1911 TO $376,000 IN 1919!

next:

BOOKER T.

IS MAGGIE WALKER'S BANK STILL GOING?

MAGGIE LENA WALKER IS THE FIRST BLACK WOMAN TO BE PRESIDENT OF A CHARTERED BANK IN AMERICA. HOWEVER, THE ST. LUKE PENNY SAVINGS BANK IS NOT HER ONLY MISSION...

THE FORMER TEACHER GIVES A $10,000 LOAN TO RICHMOND TO KEEP ITS BLACK-ONLY SCHOOLS OPEN.

IN 1921, WALKER RUNS FOR STATE SUPERINTENDENT OF PUBLIC INSTRUCTION FOR VIRGINIA. SHE LOSES BECAUSE **POLL TAXES** STOP MANY POOR BLACKS FROM VOTING.

SHE IS A BOARD MEMBER OF THE **NATIONAL ASSOCIATION FOR THE ADVANCEMENT OF COLORED PEOPLE (NAACP).** BOOKER T. WASHINGTO FOUNDER OF THE TUSKEGEE INSTITUTE, VISITS WALKER TO TALK POLITICS.

A KNEE INJURY BECOMES WORSE UNTIL SHE IS PARALYZED IN 1928. SHE PUTS A HAND-CRANKED PULLEY ELEVATOR IN HER HOUSE TO MOVE HER WHEELCHAIR.

SHE DIES IN 1934.

WALKER'S BANK SURVIVES AS THE CONSOLIDATED BANK AND TRUST COMPANY. IT IS THE OLDEST CONTINUOUS OPERATED BLACK BANK IN AMERICA! THE MONEY YOU DEPOSITED THERE IN 1903 IS WORTH MUCH MOR NO

WOW, SHE HELPED M A LOT!

THANK YOU, MAGGIE WALKE

BLOYD '01

HARRY F. BYRD SR.

Harry F. Byrd, Sr., an apple grower from the western part of Virginia, becomes **governor** and follows a **"Pay As You Go" policy for road improvements in the 1920s.** He modernizes Virginia's government offices. But he **massively resists** change when he becomes a **United States senator** for Virginia and the U.S. Supreme Court says all public schools should be **desegregated** . . .

WHO RAN "THE ORGANIZATION"?

THIS IS CHESTER "THE CRAB" TO TELL YOU ABOUT **HARRY F. BYRD SR.** HE RAN A MACHINE THAT CONTROLLED VIRGINIA POLITICS FOR THE FIRST HALF OF THE 20TH CENTURY.

WE WILL MAKE JOHN THE NEXT GOVERNOR.

I'LL PUT THE WORD OUT.

HARRY BYRD GROWS UP IN **WINCHESTER**, VIRGINIA. HIS FAMILY HAD BUILT HUGE **PLANTATIONS** IN COLONIAL TIMES.

HE IS ELECTED TO VIRGINIA'S **GENERAL ASSEMBLY** IN 1915. BYRD BECOMES GOVERNOR IN **1926**.

VIRGINIA NEEDS PAVED ROADS — BUT WE **WON'T BORROW** MONEY TO DO THE WORK.

IT'S CALLED "PAY AS YOU GO."

BYRD TAKES CONTROL OF THE DEMOCRATIC PARTY'S "ORGANIZATION." THIS **POLITICAL MACHINE** GETS DEMOCRATS ELECTED — THERE ARE **21 DEMOCRATIC** GOVERNORS IN A ROW!

HERE IS HOW BYRD WORKS IT:

① A DEMOCRAT GETS ELECTED GOVERNOR.

② THE GOVERNOR PICKS OTHER DEMOCRATS FOR BIG **STATE** JOBS.

③ THOSE POLITICIANS PICK DEMOCRATS TO RUN FOR **COUNTY** JOBS.

④ THE COUNTY OFFICIALS MAKE SURE THEIR NEIGHBORS VOTE FOR THE "ORGANIZATION" CANDIDATES. VOTERS ARE EASY TO CONTROL BECAUSE THERE ARE FEW OF THEM.

VIRGINIA CONSTITUTION of 1902

THE ORGANIZATION LAWS KEEP BLACKS FROM VOTING. A "POLL TAX" MAKES SURE VIRGINIA'S IS TOO EXPENSIVE FOR MANY BLACK VOTERS TO PAY.

BOYD '00

next: WW II

WHO SAID SEPARATE WAS UNEQUAL?

HARRY BYRD SR.'S "ORGANIZATION" KEEPS DEMOCRATS ELECTED AS LONG AS RURAL WHITE VIRGINIANS DO MOST OF THE VOTING.

POLL TAX

IN 1942, BLACK AND WHITE AMERICANS GO OVERSEAS TO FIGHT WORLD WAR II.

WE'LL TEACH THE NAZIS NOT TO HURT PEOPLE JUST BECAUSE OF THEIR RACE!

BUT WHO WILL TEACH AMERICA?

AFTER THE WAR, BLACK SOLDIERS WANT FULL CIVIL RIGHTS AT HOME.

COLORED ONLY

WHITES ONLY

THIS IS FOR THE BIRDS!

Hey, I VOTE FOR HARRY BYRD.

WHITES ONLY

COLORED ONLY

FOR THE FIRST HALF OF THE 20TH CENTURY, SEGREGATION RULES THE SOUTH. "JIM CROW" LAWS MAKE BLACKS AND WHITES GO TO SEPARATE SCHOOLS, RESTAURANTS, JOBS...

ON 1954 THE U.S. SUPREME COURT SAYS SEPARATE SERVICES ARE ALWAYS UNEQUAL IN THE CASE "BROWN VS. BOARD OF EDUCATION" FROM KANSAS:

HAVING ONE SCHOOL FOR BLACKS AND ONE FOR WHITES IS UNFAIR. PUBLIC SCHOOLS PAID FOR BY TAXES MUST BE OPEN TO EVERYONE.

SUPREME COURT

INTEGRATION?!! WHAT ABOUT STATES RIGHTS?? THE FEDERAL GOVERNMENT IS TRYING TO TELL US HOW TO RUN OUR SCHOOLS!!

BYRD, ONE OF VIRGINIA'S TWO U.S. SENATORS, IS NOT HAPPY!

BOYD '00

next: MR

WHO CREATED MASSIVE RESISTANCE?

VIRGINIA'S LEADERS ARGUE FOR TWO YEARS OVER THE U.S. SUPREME COURT'S RULING AGAINST ALL-WHITE SCHOOLS.

PLAN B
PLAN C
PLAN

WHY DON'T WE LET LOCAL SCHOOLS DECIDE IF THEY WILL INTEGRATE?

Hee Hee — MOST OF THEM WILL DECIDE **NOT** TO!

BLACK LEADERS IN THE **CIVIL RIGHTS MOVEMENT** SAY THAT IS NOT GOOD ENOUGH.

THE SUPREME COURT DECISION IS THE LAW OF THE LAND. **GET WITH IT!**

BROD '00

ON FEBRUARY **1956**, HARRY F. BYRD SR. SETS UP VIRGINIA'S MASTER PLAN...

MASSIVE RESISTANCE

WILL STOP THE SUPREME COURT ORDER! WE **WON'T** GIVE ANY STATE MONEY TO SCHOOLS THAT TEACH WHITES AND BLACKS TOGETHER!

SUPREME COURT

GULP! BYRD GETS OTHER SOUTHERN CONGRESSMEN TO AGREE TO FIGHT SCHOOL INTEGRATION! WHO WILL WIN THIS CRASH?!!

next: IMPACT!

HOW FAST DID VIRGINIA INTEGRATE?

BLACK STUDENTS ATTEND AN ALL-WHITE PUBLIC SCHOOL IN NORFOLK, VIRGINIA, FOR THE FIRST TIME ON FEB. 2, 1959.

SOME WHITES STILL TRY TO FIGHT DESEGREGATION IN LITTLE WAYS FOR 10 MORE YEARS.

SURE YOU CAN COME TO OUR SCHOOL — IF YOU CAN **WALK** THERE!

FINALLY THE U.S. SUPREME COURT HEARS A VIRGINIA CASE, "GREEN vs. SCHOOL BOARD OF NEW KENT COUNTY." THE COURT ORDERS SCHOOLS TO PROVE WITH NUMBERS THAT THEY ARE ADMITTING BLACK

21... 22... 23...

HARRY F. BYRD SR., U.S. SENATOR FROM VIRGINIA, FIGHTS THE IMPROVEMENTS TO THE CIVIL RIGHTS OF BLACKS.

YOUR **CIVIL RIGHTS ACT OF 1964** IS A MONSTER GRAB FOR POWER!

PRESIDENT LYNDON B. JOHNSON

IT STOPS **DISCRIMINATION** IN JOBS AND PUBLIC PLACES. IT PASSES!

BYRD TRIES TO STOP THE 24TH AMENDMENT TO THE CONSTITUTION.

NO MORE POLL TAXES IN FEDERAL ELECTIONS.

WE'LL KEEP THEM IN **STATE** ELECTIONS!

THE VOTING RIGHTS ACT OF **1965**...

LOOK AT ALL THESE NEW BLACK VOTERS.

I RETIRE.

WITH THE POLL TAX GONE, BYRD'S POLITICAL "ORGANIZATION" CRUMBLES. EVERYONE CAN VOTE!

AND IN 1989, I AM THE **FIRST** BLACK ELECTED TO BE GOVERNOR IN THE UNITED STATES!

L. DOUGLAS WILDER VIRGINIA

END

BOYD

18

ARTHUR ASHE

Arthur Ashe is a young **Richmond** man with the natural skills to take advantage of the **Civil Rights** progress of the 1950s. He becomes the **first African-American winner of a major men's singles tennis championship**. Ashe is also an author and eloquent speaker for social change. He coaches America's Davis Cup team against other nations in the 1980s but then gets **AIDs** and faces the toughest contest of his life . . .

WHERE DID ARTHUR ASHE GROW UP?

THIS IS THE STORY OF A SKINNY, SHY BOY NAMED **ARTHUR ASHE**. HE IS BORN JULY 10, 1943, IN THE ONLY HOSPITAL FOR BLACKS IN RICHMOND, **VIRGINIA**.

NONONO! WRONG ASH!

WHEN ARTHUR IS SIX, HIS MOM DIES. NOW ARTHUR HAS ONLY HIS FATHER AND YOUNGER BROTHER. . .

. . . AND BROOK FIELD, WHERE HIS DAD IS A POLICEMAN FOR THE PARKS DEPARTMENT.

RON CHARITY, ONE OF THE BEST BLACK TENNIS PLAYERS IN AMERICA, PRACTICES AT BROOK FIELD.

TENNIS PLAYERS HIT A BALL OVER A THREE-FOOT-HIGH NET. THEY TRY TO HIT THE BALL INTO THE OPPONENT'S SPACE WITHOUT HIM RETURNING IT.

YOU PLAY TENNIS? I CAN TEACH YOU.

ARTHUR IS SMALL BUT QUICK — A BOOST IN TENNIS. HE PRACTICES A LOT.

AT 10, ARTHUR GOES TO LYNCHBURG TO TRAIN WITH DR. WALTER JOHNSON. JOHNSON HELPS BLACKS LEARN TO PLAY TENNIS — WHICH SOME CALL A "WHITE MAN'S GAME."

YOUR BACKHAND IS VITAL! SO IS BEING CALM AND POLITE ON THE TENNIS COURT.

next: **BEST MAN** ON **CAMPUS**

HOW DID ARTHUR ASHE PLAY BETTER?

THIS IS THE STORY OF ARTHUR ASHE, A GREAT TENNIS PLAYER FROM RICHMOND, VIRGINIA.

ARTHUR WINS MANY TOURNAMENTS IN STATES NEAR VIRGINIA. SOME EVENT ORGANIZERS REFUSE TO LET HIM PLAY BECAUSE OF HIS SKIN COLOR.

IN THE 1950S, AMERICA IS STRUGGLING WITH **INTEGRATION** – HAVING BLACK AND WHITE PEOPLE PLAY, WORK, AND LIVE TOGETHER.

AT 17, HE IS ONE OF THE BEST BLACK TENNIS PLAYERS IN AMERICA.

HE SPENDS HIS SENIOR YEAR OF HIGH SCHOOL IN ST. LOUIS, MISSOURI TO GET A BETTER TENNIS COACH.

GOOD! ATTACK MORE!

IN 1961, HE WINS A UNITED STATES LAWN TENNIS ASSOCIATION CHAMPIONSHIP. HE IS THE BEST MALE HIGH SCHOOL PLAYER -- OF ANY SKIN COLOR.

ASHE ATTENDS THE UNIVERSITY OF CALIFORNIA AT LOS ANGELES (UCLA).

PRACTICE, PRACTICE, PRACTICE GETS HIM **A 130** MPH SERVE!

IN 1965 HE HELPS UCLA WIN THE COLLEGE TENNIS CHAMPIONSHIP.

RICHMOND OFFICIALS DECLARE FEB. 4, **1966** "ARTHUR ASHE DAY."

THE CITY THAT WAS ONCE THE CAPITAL OF THE CONFEDERACY NOW HONORS A DESCENDANT OF SLAVES. WHAT A TURNAROUND!

BOYD '01

next: IS SOUTH AFRICA OPEN?

WHO WON THE FIRST U.S. OPEN?

As ARTHUR ASHE GETS OLDER, HE PLAYS TENNIS EVEN BETTER.

IN 1968, ASHE ENTERS THE **FIRST** UNITED STATES OPEN TENNIS TOURNAMENT. HE REACHES THE SEMI-FINALS TO PLAY CLARK GRAEBNER.

CLARK IS PLAYING CAREFULLY, WAITING FOR ME TO MESS UP!

I AM STILL GOING TO HIT MY TRICKY SHOTS!

ASHE BEATS GRAEBNER AND THEN BEATS HOLLAND'S TOM OKKER TO WIN THE U.S. OPEN!

WINNING THE OPEN HELPS MAKE ASHE THE TOP-RANKED MALE TENNIS PLAYER IN THE WORLD IN 1968.

HIS WIN IS PART OF A TIME OF NEW ACHIEVEMENTS FOR BLACKS. MANY MARCH TO WIN **CIVIL RIGHTS.** OLYMPIC ATHLETES GIVE "BLACK POWER" SALUTES.

THIS SAME YEAR, ASHE AND OTHER AMERICANS WIN THE DAVIS CUP IN AUSTRALIA. ON THEIR WAY HOME THEY VISIT U.S. SOLDIERS FIGHTING IN **VIETNAM.**

THIS... WAR IS A WASTE OF LIVES!

ASHE BECOMES MORE AWARE OF WORLD PROBLEMS AS HE TRAVELS TO TENNIS MATCHES. IN 1973 HE IS THE **FIRST** BLACK TO PLAY THE SOUTH AFRICA OPEN. SOUTH AFRICA HAS "APARTHEID," WHICH SEPARATES BLACKS AND WHITES. (REMEMBER HOW U.S. LAW DID THAT WHEN ASHE GREW UP IN VIRGINIA?)

• FOR EUROPEANS ONLY •

THIS ISN'T AS BAD AS I READ ABOUT... IT IS **WORSE!!**

next: WIMBLEDON WIN

WHY DID ARTHUR ASHE STOP PLAYING?

IN 1979, 36-YEAR-OLD TENNIS STAR ARTHUR ASHE HAS A HEART ATTACK. HE CANNOT PLAY TENNIS AGAIN UNLESS HE HAS SURGERY TO REPAIR HIS HEART.

HE HAS THE SURGERY.

A YEAR LATER, WHILE JOGGING TO GET STRONGER, ASHE HAS ANOTHER HEART ATTACK.

HE GETS ANOTHER HEART OPERATION IN 1983. A BLOOD TRANSFUSION GIVES HIS BODY SOME NEW BLOOD TO HELP HIM RECOVER.

ASHE CANNOT PLAY TENNIS ANYMORE. HE STILL LOVES THE GAME AND COACHES AMERICA'S DAVIS CUP TEAM FROM 1981 TO 1985. AMERICA WINS IN 1981 AND 1982.

ASHE ALSO PROTESTS THE DISCRIMINATORY GOVERNMENT OF SOUTH AFRICA. HE IS ARRESTED IN 1985 FOR PROTESTING ITS LAWS AGAINST BLACKS.

FREE SOUTH AF...

IN 1992 ASHE REVEALS THAT HE HAS HIV, THE VIRUS THAT CAUSES AIDS. ASHE GOT IT FROM INFECTED BLOOD IN THE TRANSFUSION AFTER HIS 1983 HEART SURGERY.

I WILL SPEND THE REST OF MY LIFE HELPING OTHERS FIGHT AIDS.

ASHE DIES OF AN AIDS-RELATED ILLNESS ON FEB. 6, 1993. HE IS BURIED IN RICHMOND, VIRGINIA.

IN 1996, A STATUE OF HIM GOES ON RICHMOND'S MONUMENT AVENUE AFTER A BIG DEBATE. ASHE NOW STANDS NEAR STATUES OF CIVIL WAR CONFEDERATE SOLDIERS WHO FOUGHT FOR STATES THAT PRACTICED SLAVERY.

END